JOHN STOKES' HORSE

JOHN STOKES' HORSE

Peter Sanger

GASPEREAU PRESS LIMITED

PRINTERS & PUBLISHERS

MMXII

FOR M.

CONTENTS

JOHN STOKES' HORSE

FISHING FOR JADE

the poet wrestles with the horses in his brain
LORCA

𝄢 CLEF

Here
at a glance
the rhythmic line
adheres.

Sweet
harmony,
how do you like
this air

on
a flute
worth a sou,
on a penny

whistle?
It is trying
to speak
cantabile.

Do you have
the companions,
the fool, the hero,
the singer,

the dog or
frog who will
save the day,
the tree

of light
in the prow?
Let light
administer light.

The moon is
still moored
beside
Africa.

Here is a pot
of red ochre.
Reach me your
hand. We'll begin.

Hard helm. The ship's Ptolemaic pivot
   spins world around it:
sea, stars, moon, backscatter
   light along the night shore,

excessive light, light
   reflected from light,
the ship's light returned
   as unbreakable code,

psalm, hymn, prayer
   deferred by a turn in the culture.
Such pelagic business. Each ship shall proceed
   at safe speed, avoid

collision, assess fog, waves, rain
   and all previous vision,
small rocking boats of primitive faith,
   now invisible truth.

Part clay, part glass,
part snapped
from a poet's cup
of universal pyrex.

Lost then found
in a poet's abandoned garden,
skim-milk white it's bound
not to shine like a dove's neck

or a biblical rainbow.
No more any matter of substance
than descants
by shadow.

Lift it up.
Let it pass from you,
invisible cup
unheld by this handle.

Drink from a fracture.
Stoop to earth
and babbling gelall, gelall,
taste strait air.

Take a lantern. Go looking
for light beyond the Great Wall.
Send a message abroad
though the news is at home: no smell,

taste, touch, thought, no eyes,
ears, nose, tongue, no form, no sound,
but sea silver now in moonlight,
the moon rising full, round,

white, a pearl, a seed,
and this, a thumb's length of green
grey glaze, a goddess of clay,
the hearer of cries, Kuan Yin,

whose body so slightly incised
is almost no more than a volute
of water concealing her
hood, face, arms, thighs. Her left

hand is holding a chalice
of dew as if each morning
were mercy, love, beauty, grace.
She forgives illusory hearing,

shadows pursuing shadow,
for whom nothing, the nameless,
is always beginning, while deer
shape nests in the grass.

Leaves veined by gold
   petals defined
by gold-painted edges,

pink and vermilion
   flowers joined
by a random net

of jointed stalks,
   two birds in ochre
bibs and blue tuckers

fly between brook
   and cloud. This
appearance of things

occurs when things wish
   and when we may
see them. A painter

might find their inner line
   when two birds still
call after flying

away to a third. "I look
   for notes that love
one another," said Mozart.

Then she put my hand
   upon moon's reflection,
not there, in the water.

Of a size to contain
    five grains of rice
or a sip of green tea
    they're thimbles
fit for no thumbs.

Light, a quick touch,
    and glaze
upon one becomes craquelure
    under two scarlet
starbursts of aster.

A second is smoothly slipped
    cream whose scarves
of cerise flow loosely afloat
    as if water still
moves in their colour.

The third takes a fortunate
    flaw, a sprackle
of kiln fleck, budding boughs
    with pink blossom,
green leaves in relief.

Ask me, love, what we've
      been given. Start
in the centre, encompassing
      outward. Brush
yourself over the brim.

Another small bowl of light,
continuing still, allowing
the art of making things
make themselves around it.

Decahedral, red, blue,
gold, ignitions of pheonix
across double panels,
iris, peony, two

aureate deer lie
lifting throats to feed
on blossoming plum.
"Interesting is easy,"

said Mahler to Walter,
"beautiful difficult."
And you may believe
in the purr

of a courting toad,
in a dragonfly's summer
wedding, ceremonious
as a woodland orchid,

in a cricket's sabbath
concert, in the dance
where butterflies match
their cells of silk and earth.

Nothing is like. Rattle
of leaves in fall
is like nothing so much as
rattle of leaves in fall

or the strange bird in spring, buff
breast, blue back, cheek patch
yellow, perched in a glaze
of sky and earth.

When heart is at ease,
hand swift,
first draw its beak
then its eyes.

Draw its head and half
of its wings. Fletch primaries in.
Colour rufous its tail.
Cast it off

to fly among blossom,
three blossoms and two, painted
by brush strokes like raindrops,
tipped pink into plum,

where all through winter
it rides its weight
up by down, empty
on one sprig of air.

For the sake of the sacred
    instruments, for the discs
of heaven and earth,
    for tablets

inscribed with black
    varnish conferring
immortality upon
    the ancestors,

for girdle pendants,
    crescents, rings
which make known
    intentions, display

ability and signify
    capability deciding
questions of aversion
    or doubt, for sonorous

stones, strung and suspended
    from frames, struck
with a hammer to mark
    divisions in verse,

for stones in the grave
    sealing eyes, lips, ears,
navel to ensure their
    function continue,

I go fishing for jade
    in a glacial river
stripped to the quick,
    wading water,

without hook or net,
    step by step,
feeling for water-worn
    jade, the touch

of its skin unexpected,
    no way of securing
it happen again,
    life's motion,

the colour of jade
    mottled red, milk
white, yellow brown
    with black streaks,

cloud patterns, but
    I cannot make
inventory, the colours
    too various

and would have to include
    the lost hue "merdacas"
whose stone cost the Khan
    four cities

before disappearing, its
    dust mixed with rice,
apt food
    for the dead.

No-one is with him.
No-one watches from lion-
coloured hills while
he digs in dry grass.

Don't pity this dreamer.
He couldn't choose
what to dream. As usual,
a dream chose him.

He might be digging
his grave while a grave
executioner standing
beside him tests

a blade against air.
But no-one stands by him.
His spade cuts sod,
sand, clay. It picks

apart puzzles of slate.
Perhaps he is halfway
to China. It seems so,
the dryness, the dust,

the lion-coloured hills
and the sudden brocade
of a shroud
in the pit he is digging,

red, black, gold,
sublunary stars,
chrysanthemum petals
spilled onto

his hands while silk
is unfolding,
untarnished, unstained,
uncovering

a body armoured
in jade, a plastron
quilted with tablets
of jade, a shimmering

greeness, phosphorescent
as plankton, a voice
saying this
is the final chrysalis.

Hippocampus, not hippo-
potamus. The ark
didn't bounce and recover
one handsbreadth of freeboard
when you disembarked. If
Lamarck was right, by then
you'd refused the task
we now assume of being invariably
big. You flipped
yourself over the rail,
rode the tail of a salty brook
swallowing itself into ocean.

Unlikely as art, or the size
of a thumbnail sketch,
you keep the continuous arch
of a chess knight. All your
moves are upright, steering
by two rounded fins where your neck
swells down into what might
have been shoulder if you'd had
our recourse to arms. Instead,
you inhabit eelgrass and seaweed
where we might observe you approach
an amphipod in a casual manner,

peer at it a second or two
and placing your pipestem snout
in the most convenient position
suddenly engulf your meal. You
are said by those with the patience
to listen to make a monotonous sound
akin to that of a tambour
which becomes (understandably so) more
intense and frequent in breeding season
when a female deposits one hundred
and fifty eggs in a male's
ventral brood pouch. This marsupial

solution makes you fish, bird,
mammal. Practising such finesse
why did you ever reject
the amphibian? A male marsupial
who carries all her eggs in his basket
could only have had an enviable future.
As it is, you're seaside prelude to Ovid,
and we also did best to begin by inventing
Westminister Abbey. Later times will find
leisure and bombs to destroy it.
Sea pony, salt crystal, gallop me home,
mare, maris, marriage-maker.

RHUBARB

Somewhere between fruit and vegetable
　　you're almost proof
of spontaneous combustion, fisting
　　red knuckles through mud
during snowdrifts.

I admire your local tumescence
　　at well-managed feasts,
pied, squared, jammed, stewed,
　　though you make thin wine.
For a pillar of water emitting

red shreds of acid you grow
　　with tasteful bravura,
democratic but also prepared
　　to set teeth
on edge in a frisson

of fastidious hauteur. I've
    often found you incult
in a plot behind the stone cellar
    of some vanished farmhouse,
seeding each year, ticking over,

steady as words in Victorian
    narrative poetry.
Winter, your stalks are bleached out,
    speckled by melanin
pigment, pithless, all struck agley

in a rout of abandoned pipes
    diskiltered by weather.
Breathing sound through one is no
    sorrow and sigh too near to
the wind's to grieve at and magnify.

INDIAN PIPE

(*Monotropa uniflora*)

An opaque lexicographer
    might still see you
double, but for most of us
    now your metaphor

hardly adheres. Penny
    clay pipes in a fabular
wilderness tavern aren't
    referent reality.

Like language you've
    simply continued,
outlive the seemingly solid,
    kicked-stone proof

to be only yourself, so
    it seems. Using no
chlorophyll, your consequence
    isn't albino.

At a distance you stand,
    a handsized cluster
of vertical stems, white
    as if frost had

covered them. But up close
each resolves to translucence,
sheathed by small pointed
bracts that compose

at the tip of each stem,
white and hanging recurved,
the minute bell
of one blossom.

Once was a poet
who picked you and named
you "preferred flower of life."
She dressed in white

and awoke into dispossession,
writing "maturity only
enhances mystery, never
decreases it." Illusion,

ghost flower, turning black
as your single fruits ripen,
there's no turning back,
turning back.

SHATTERGLASS

Once when I held
   a mirror to nature
aloft on a bureau's
   gimbal

in the box of my pickup
   off up the road
from a secondhand sale,
   my truck

hit a bump and the mirror
   winged. O, I saw
it all happen. My
   side mirror

caught it, the smash
   on macadam, then
airborne
   a pattern

of fragments, another
   coherence,
an unlocking jigsaw
   of ancient

nostalgia, trees,
   leaves, flowers,
sky, exploding
   together

in final brilliance,
   and yes, is it
poetry if nothing
   rhymes?

Something must sing
   and almost despair
at the time
   at the time.

How can I live
without blossom
of sweet laburnum?

A stillness
in the ravine,
incandescent,

coals
turning colder,
lignite.

Some music
knows
its own past

and what is
to come,
far worse

than the worst
we've ever
experienced.

CIVICS

I knew horseplay, knew it for a murderous thing.
W.B. YEATS

Yes, since you ask, I've seen
another Troy: a worm
extending, contracting in rhythms
of desperate propulsion

just ahead of a beetle
pistoning murder
on slender feet, whose antennae
are subtle,

whose mandibles bear
small need of magnification,
who will live immortal
years. Nature

makes art of a kind.
If the worm were Hector
or beetle Achilles, I
hadn't mind

to decide in time.
As witnesses say, things
happened too fast to prevent,
though not, later, rhyme.

In the capital city
of another language,
two decades before
the dictator fell,
I discovered
my librairie.

It opened at one
on Sundays, so I
sat on the curb
and waited. At
quarter to one
some dozen men

sauntering singly
down otherwise empty
streets arrived
also to wait. Cement
apartments were
looking. They

were ordered to look.
Silent, we filed
into the shop
where all
except me
took up a book

and started to read.
I saw a foxed copy
of Verlaine's *Sagesse* locked
in a case, gestured to see it.
The readers stopped reading
while seeming to read.

A quiet bleak
man unlocking a case
handed me Verlaine's *Sagesse*
(too much, far more than the nothing
I could afford). He smiled
when he locked the book

back. The dictator's wife
approved executions.
She liked to wear
her white lab coat
proposing
a final narrative.

CIVICS

(Autumn 2010 – Spring 2011)

I.

On the walls of Solomon's Lane
I found two signs of the times:
RIP SAM, KILLA KALI.

They never moved while I
patrolled the steps. They never
said who dribbled them there.

God in His wisdom puts
leaves into air. A bomb went off
under the archduke's carriage.

II.

What do you mean "archduke"? We're
all Canadian now. "You people too,"
says our man in the tar pit.

Wasn't Sam some serial killer,
Killa Kali a rapster? That fits.
Friends, we're here in St. John's,

up Solomon's Lane, just
like the Bible. "To be perfectly
frank," he said, "I personally

feel there are times when capital
punishment is appropriate. But I'm
not, you know, in the next parliament

I'm not, no plans to bring that issue
forward." Trust him. He covers
his basis. Con speak. Barratry

casual, equivocal predicates,
statecraft procuring the gloat
of Narcissus. Word city, St. John's,

do you still loft an eagle, speech
in free jurisdiction? Scribbling
voices mark the waste land.

III.

Le premier ministre speaks
in plain English for ordinary
Canadians. Extraordinary ones

don't get it. They'll get it.
So much for them. How do
the ordinary rule the extraordinary?

By bagmen, facemen, spinners and weavers.
By ten odd years of civil amnesia.
By persecution and slander of all evidentiaries

until they seem guilty.
The requisite language is
perfectly frank. To be

perfectly frank is requisite
language. See how
journalists run.

See how they run. The rush
is addictive. Where did you hide
your night? Under what bushel.

IV.

That our soldiers come home
as survivors not victors
for we honour the dead

by more dying. That we keep
our contracts unbroken
for the sake of the contracted.

That our treasure be spent,
for it is treasure's nature
to be expended, as also

the nature of blood. That
sacrifice be not in vain for our
politicians promote vanity.

That by lies and concealment
freedom is made inevitable.
That tyranny is only

a transitional necessity. That we
torture because we're
tormented. That the people be happy.

V.

Eyes that preside with equal stare
at the opening of ice rinks
and the ceremony of soldiers

maimed and mad. Unaccountable eyes
staring unmoved on the never
called to account. Transparent

eyes backed by a foil of opaqueness.
Eyes to see through you. Eyes
boundless and bare with the calibrate

focus of wolf and coyote. Eyes
of predation so pure that innocence
thinks evil its only salvation.

VI.

Attention. This is the great Canadian
monotone. This is the level voice
of a straight shooter. As for you,

you're dead, unless you pulled the trigger,
unless you're part of the gang,
unless you're a lickspittle bully

whose tumbling gabble blusters
ways through facts and questions,
unless you collaborate. "I am

horrified of the German voices.
They betray absolutely everything,
they cry out their own evil,"

wrote Haecker in 1940. Against
the monotone of authority,
opposition compromised, dissent

divided, freedom mortgaged
to infinite globality, only
Kierkegaard's "silent despair"?

VII.

Wonderful time. You are here.
Lies in the quicklime. Evil
a market commodity.

What shall it profit when iron
is cut from its mountain,
when oil is transhumed from its soil,

when salmon lose way in the ocean,
when rivers are silted deltas,
when whales cannot sound

when butterflies dry into paper,
when bees become husks in their hives?
Shall nighthawks coast dusk,

shall swallows split air
with their axes, shall snipe
return to the meadow

and flying tight curves at evening,
make Japanese flutes
from their wings?

VIII.

Flute of deliverance
after the shadows
have died by fire:

this is the park
of the son of heaven.
Samples, symbols

are walking its paths.
In its glades are
sun dappled beasts.

A tree at its centre
is stave for the emperor's
nightingale, or

that's what one story
says. No wonder
the teller of stories

is laughing,
earth being more
than one way to speak.

GARDENER

(i.m., J. C-N., murdered while teaching French)

Against death dressed in black,
against a poor, cold mammet
with clips of used out cliché
clicked into the grips
of his Glock and Walther,
hollow-point, hollow,

straddled from target to target
aiming at zero, the central
projectile himself,
the final faceoff,
the achieved copy.
Against death dressed in black

Michaelmas daisies so common
they grow all over the fields.
She planted them there, there,
careful clumps in her garden
because, as she said, they
are so beautiful.

Honeysuckle in bloom
that October, and when I
asked how, she mimed plucking
spent blossoms six hours
for one day with faith
flowers would follow,

for she had a gardener's patience.
Against death dressed in black
I remember her speaking French,
three or four words recorded
on tape, replayed in the spin
of a week's media elegy,

and one word caught back
from the wrap of voice-over
cover, pronounced exact
facets, "l'éducation,"
leading forth, abiding away
from her garden.

⫷ FRAGMENTS OF WALL

Truro, Nova Scotia, 11 September 2011

    I.

Like emergency powers, even this wall
   seems to have turned domestic:
unmegalithic, six rectangular
   slabs brought in ballast
across the Atlantic to dress up
   a line facing Prince Street.

    II.

Rusty rebar pokes through their cement
   in places where sledgehammer,
crowbar, scoop of a backhoe,
   swing and thud
of a wrecking ball opened a surface
   to stains of old blood.

III.

Once was a year we were all
    Berliners. I can't remember
it well. Are these slabs souvenirs
    or civil memorials? No signage.
Just a plot between buildings, petunias, grass,
    slabs attempting Stonehenge.

IV.

In a literate age there are
    always graffiti, but here
there is only one, not *frei*
    scrawled by a hand furtively
hidden behind no-one's back to the wall,
    but *fraise*, strawberry.

V.

Who could be shot writing in French
   strawberry? Call it
freedom, which might also
   explain the washes of palest pink,
blue, purple paint, fading now,
   and allow one to think

VI.

it was absence of love took
   this wall down, a weight
without function, losing context.
   Touch your tongue to its old cement.
Taste everywhere now
   sea's original salt.

ARTEMISIA

(Easter Sunday, 2011)

Mother of herbs, hallowed once
to the lady of beasts,
Diana,

bitter friend, virgin sister
to fire-robed
Apollo,

I've tasted waters you
made bitter, though there's
dust on your leaf

or a semblance of dust
on its glabrous surface.
Perhaps it recalls

Tartarian steppes where you're
said to abound. I'll
never see them.

The last time I looked
you resisted
all metaphor.

Is your bitterness always
healing? Must we drink
the dry iron

of your blood though ceding
your Greek to invocative
mugwort,

to wormwood, not dust
in an urn sealed
from time?

Is it all
a matter
of listening?

Unless you
speak
I've nothing

to say. When
you've said
robins

in late
afternoon
sing

rainbows
inside their
throats

do I
hear you
rightly?

Which side
of that echo
are we?

JOHN STOKES' HORSE

*The horse of the mind must submit to the harness of
the word, of the metre: otherwise it would lose its way*

ROBERTO CALASSO

JOHN STOKES' HORSE

I.

Get back on your horse.
Bring forth buds. Bloom blossom.
Yield almonds whose shell
is bitter and kernel sweet.

Leave instruments
of the solitary and studious:
spheres, quadrants, sextants,
laurels, myrtles

and similar novelties.
Fountains are not
always philanthropic.
Horses must drink.

II.

Here is a background:
Pegasus knocking a hoof
into Helicon, Christmas
under the tree,

a matter of inches,
sixteen by twelve
carved into shape
by a jacknife.

Piebald protector of dreams,
star-leaper, moon-grazer,
sun-chariot,
sorry nag.

III.

A small wooden horse,
brown and white,
carved for a grandson
in 1907.

Primitive art, a buckle
of leather around its neck
and over its shoulders
for me to hang onto.

Carved from whatever
God knows, pine, spruce,
tamarack, thickety
tuckamore.

IV.

In dreams, in visions,
riding a calico toy,
I'm only a child dressed
this brief while in eternity.

One horse is a horse.
Two horses are horses.
This is the horse
of John Stokes.

With better eyes,
with supple fingers,
with a sharper knife,
I never could carve you.

v.

These may also be words.
Push the peg in one shoulder
and rise. Twist the screw
in the other and fall.

Turn yourself by the reins.
Sound, sound, between three worlds,
you can't ride an ebony horse
but a whittle of air.

Is that what you mean
by real? Noble
ignoble, Verrocchio's hack
reduced to some plinth.

VI.

Generous wood. A child's
hand may warm it.
Gallop, trot, walk
at a wish, at a wish.

Spin a new tail and tell me.
This horse is of passing
swiftness, engendered
by wind and flame.

Canter a counterweave
silence. Pass by,
mother of worlds,
pursuivant of vanished Troy.

VII.

Bleak noble rider,
here begins terror,
here begins miracle.
Pack ice rucks

on Cape Freels,
floaters and sinkers.
Spring's dry grass will
explode into black incendiary.

One winter, no horse,
I hauled out wood
with a handsled.
Alder, all flashout and ash.

VIII.

This horse and rider
shall part the sea,
a Marah of bitter
water. Only Elim is sweet.

As for the riding,
keep it casual.
Folk art: I don't believe.
John Stokes' horse.

Broken light, broken the way,
broken the simple saying.
Aerolith, angel of stone,
I've tried to stick with you.

IX.

Let reins fall loose
on its neck. Let it take
what road it chooses.
Let it leap the ford

and the burning mountain.
Kill it and clothe yourself
in its skin. Preserve
its flesh from corruption.

Twice to be born, who
else can it be but you,
steed, nag, perambulant toy,
horse knowing more than the gods.

X.

The horse is the dream of horses
as the song is the dream of songs,
not of their singer. Hoofed with psalms
it gallops beyond

moon's equivocation.
One of a kind, on August nights,
its hide is that shimmering
out by the chains of Andromeda.

Loyalty gone, kinship gone,
at the end of the world
will be sounds of furious riding.
Its muzzle will dip, drink.

XI.

"Come on Mummy, let's cross the road."
First words. First sentence.
And there on the other side
of the street of a village in England,

bay-coloured and glistening,
trotting a tightrope of muscle
in sunlight, that great bay horse
carried its noble rider,

neck like the bow of Ulysses
re-curved for a killing
before innocence mattered
and I lived in the colour of singing.

XII.

I knew the words by the picture
when my mother read, before I could
read and re-read that page
where wind blew through leaves

and I looking up from the book,
heard wind blowing through leaves,
and promised to find right words
wind made through the real leaves.

O, I'd ride such a canter of words
until they and my horse
were one
pond, frog, splash.

XIII.

Is yours the head
a knacker nailed
upon the gateway wall?
Dear Falada,

who spoke as if my
mother knew her heart
would break in two,
I'm here. I hear.

I've braided all my hair.
The false bride's in a barrel
with spikes. Chopped is your head
upon the gateway wall.

XIV.

Climb the climbing wave
so the sea can break
beneath laurel oars
of Virgil.

What city is left
to be a sacred geometry?
One bar of music
may be all that is blessed.

Still in the saddle,
stay still in the saddle.
I might get it much better
but that's not likely to happen.

XV.

There we all were, Chatham
Ontario. Best news in town
was the iced little leap
of Barbara Ann Scott.

A clip-clopping horse
delivered milk
from a rubber-tired wagon
along Victoria Avenue.

Its reins were slack on the hames.
The route was invariable.
The curb I remember
was always a munch of oats.

XVI.

Word for word: reins can be
kicked in the gut as well
as, yes, it's a wet one. Do I
make myself clear? Some are

borne natural like Arabian horses
on wings. Softer than moss
is the nap of their muzzles,
strict clatter of hooves

when they land in the casbah.
Piebald dobbin slods up
down the shore with a slide
of slithering seaweed.

XVII.

Abdulla on a white mare
came softly, bevied
by richly-armed slaves
on foot about him.

An Arabian child. Out of
Titania, by Bottom. By
Titania, out of Bottom.
I almost see

through half-closed eyes
mistily things of essential
radiance. Summers living
by stone, winter, ice.

XVIII.

Let dogs leap into stone
tearing marble flanks
of Actaeon. I'm
on this horse

and love on me
at one in the dressage.
Strange work to prove
a horseman to horse,

a horse to love.
The man has to have
his mare again
that all might be well.

XIX.

Sleipnir has eight legs.
So what.
Four are enough for me.
I'll run them off.

Iambic quadrameter.
No-one writes it.
Rare as sapphics.
Why should I care,

or you for that matter?
Except the rein holds
one way winter
when frost bends grass.

xx.

That ammoniac smell,
the flicker of muscles
flexing its skin,
scattering deer flies.

Pity a tired wooden horse.
Pity the child who imagined
it easy to ride, hoofed with psalms,
beyond the equivocal moon.

Eidolon Helen was always
absent in Egypt.
Rings on her fingers,
she goes, she goes, she goes.

XXI.

You had to be there. The pass
was not really a pass. It angled
a mountain. You leaned
on a mountain to climb.

We bucked the horses
through snow. The snow
became ice. At first we
stepped over the horses,

then we stepped on them,
then we stepped through them.
You had to be there to see.
Someone took pictures.

XXII.

Do Castor and Pollux
couch spears beside you?
Do you charge for the hearth
of Vesta, charge

for the Golden Shield?
Will the gods live
for ever? Are the Twins
on your side today?

The blades are all in a line.
Kandahar, and would you
believe, as after Vimy,
no hoofprint in flint.

XXIII.

He said to me, he said to me,
a poem must carry
some measure of grief.
Was this what he meant?

He'll not speak a third time.
He's dead. Poor, tired, old
horse, how did you carry on?
How you did carry on.

One hoof at a time
through wind and rain.
In the scald of fission
shadows adhere to the wall.

XXIV.

A frayed rope tail,
remnants of rope
for a mane. And so,
sweet harmonies,

how do you like this air?
Let in the daemon
whenever the music's
daemonic.

Not mimesis, but moments
the world is beside itself,
the dove whose call
is elsewhere and here.

XXV.

One, two, three, this is the horse
whose tallest leap will reach
the top of the tallest tower
by the dark sea at Trebizond

where a princess waits
in a firebird bower for the tallest
kiss in the tallest tower
by the dark sea at Trebizond.

Pray for your father's ashes.
He'll call from the grave three times.
Ivan shall have his Helena.
The dark mare is mine.

XXVI.

Last laugh. A horse laugh,
lips nickered back. Toothless.
No nips. Soft muzzle of moss.
Bolt the door. It has gone

to remain as a gift
on another Ionian shore,
myth never being the question
it answers. It stacks

an army inside. Wise
wooden horse, all your
riders are ridden, reborn
as the child at your thigh.

XXVII.

Always at night I remember
the slow thump of hoofbeats
on summer pasture.
I'd wake to walk

where the shape of horses
was darker darkness
than darkness and suddenly
only a touch away,

close summer shadows that moved
upon speaking hooves,
bread and wine for Elias
ascending in fire one heaven.

XXVIII.

When is now, as when
the white horse
leaping at random
against its hobble

galloped out on the steppe
to join its nightdrifting herd.
That's not my memory,
or the voice which spoke

from wind's embrasure
before staying mute ten years.
White horse, dark horse,
whinny, all whicker and huff.

XXIX.

Proteus, the changeful,
still rides the sea.
I'll ride this wooden horse.
Its heartbeat's a pulse in my ear

and the soft clash of bronze.
Always so borne,
the time between time,
the time's incarnation.

A life of deciphering shadow.
How else could I see the sun?
Time to move on. Beg me
a dollar for Charon.

XXX.

Has the horse made John Stokes
or Stokes made the horse?
I say the horse was made
with love and heart's understanding.

Early by late and every year often
his was a song of degrees
carving an outline in air
for John Stokes' grandson.

Anchises has slipped
from my shoulders.
There's no imperial pathos.
Open, dark gates of Erebus.

XXXI.

Tell me to take
life as it comes,
in whatever
whittled way.

Do you mean single-
cut carving? Form
released by one stroke
from an odd stick of kindling?

Mane running
with the grain,
nostrils, eyes, ears
sconces of flame.

XXXII.

Picking your way, one wave
at a time from comber
to comber, by lightning flashes,
or striking sparks

from the cobble, riding fire
until it is smoke
and you are horse-
headed Demeter

alone in her cave, grieving
for lost Persephone, the horse
of the dead, the horse
of the yet to be born.

XXXIII.

Saddle up. This isn't a Western.
Capriole, vault, curvet,
just whisper the horseman's word.
It's not in the Bible.

Own it, and all will be Eden.
Imagine the rider as child,
a bubble in spirit, balanced,
with level hands. The horse

hauling wood and the wooden horse
are the same. That's
a secret for centaurs. I
seem to be saying goodbye.

XXXIV.

In winter his bedroom was cold.
A mouthful of air puffed over the quilt
made the word steam.
He could neigh like a horse.

He practised. On Christmas Day
in the morning he beat out
the old wooden stairs to find
a wood horse under the popcorn tree.

Wood was its skin and smelt
of grandfather's pipe. It couldn't
whuff steam in the air. It couldn't
neigh. He started to practise.

XXXV.

These wake nights I think of him,
the hobby horse man, his stiff-legged
prance like Mr. Scissors, his grandmotherly
swaddle of quilts and taffeta twirls.

Other signs I know:
the ermine's ghazals, the ptarmigan's
feathered triads, the hare's
discursive quatrains. Not the trackless

child who once kept watch
by his window, then secretly
mounting his steed ran off
into snow and evergreen darkness.

LEAPING TIME

Poetry should be like horse racing;
wild horses, with jockeys made of marble,
an unseen finish line lies hidden in the clouds

ADAM ZAGAJEWSKI

THEY WERE THERE BEFORE HE WAS: three white ducks with yellow beaks. They were silhouettes cut from thin board. The first duck was big, the second, middling. The third duck was smallest. They led a life of precise procession, each glued onto its own painted platform green as pond water, travelling on cotton spool wheels. The platforms were joined by rubber hinges, one to two, two to three.

Theoretically, because of the rubber hinges, the procession should have been able to turn corners. In practice, if he pulled the string attached to the biggest, leading duck any other way than straight the lined procession toppled over. A lesson was involved that he was never to learn.

He both was and was not the smallest duck. Its position seemed most desirable, a mix of security and liberty. He, when he was it, could leave the procession at will by simply dropping out, or he, it, could stay and by bringing up the end of the procession make it complete, one, two, three. But he also pulled the string, which it was obvious the littlest duck could not pull. He was living the contradictions and grandeurs of his first metaphor, a metaphor that lived. When he started being fed with a spoon, he would not eat until the spoonfuls were first offered in turn to ducks one, two, three. It would be a nice matter to decide if politics or charity was the issue. Whatever the case (perhaps both were in play), the play was serious. Those ducks lived.

Junkers 87's and 88's sometimes flew over the village where he dwelled on their way to or from bombing raids to the northeast and northwest, to Birmingham, Liverpool, Sheffield, Leeds, Coventry. They gave flesh to or tried to destroy the flesh of other metaphors not entirely distant from his parade of wooden ducks trundling like pre-Carolingian kings in painted carts. On clear, still nights, as his parents later told him, the Junkers' engines pulsed with doppleresque monotonies, wave after wave, and firestorms were visible from the burning cities a hundred or so miles away fluttering in the night sky (he later had to imagine) like northern lights. But he never heard the engines or saw the firestorms because he had no words to single either out from the nameless, unanticipatable, ungeneralized phenomena of the world in which he was immersed, no way of saying what they were like or unlike.

It was the custom of his country to put young children to bed often and early. He was an only child. His mother was also an only child, one who had lost her mother by heart failure while still young. His father was often away, and perhaps she found the company of a small child in a lonely cottage, in a village where she had no friends and no method of getting about but walking, bewildering, tiring and trying her patience. After dinner at noon (the largest meal of the day), he was shut up in his bedroom until four o'clock. Then he was given what was called an afternoon tea of perhaps buttered, often margarined bread and a glass of milk, diluted canned milk. Then, after a great, central event of his day, he was led or carried back to his bed again by six-thirty.

During those long afternoons and seemingly unending English summer twilights, he seldom slept. He watched wind blow the curtains and leaf shadows shiver and dash on the plaster walls. His bed was an iron framed cot. Its mattress was protected by oilcloth. All his life he would remember its faintly uric and sharply carbolic smell and the contradictions of its surface, hot, cold, dry, wet, slippery and sticky. The ducks were not with him. He would have talked with them, not slept. Once, when he was very young, he felt a sudden giving-way in the cloth around his middle while he lay on the bed, and a dark gruel ran out of him. He used it to make patterns on the wall, and then there was suddenly shouting and his body was lifted and fell down on the oilcloth.

His companions while he did not sleep were himself and, in the summer the flies, cabbage moths and cabbage moth caterpillars who came through the screenless open window of the wall alongside his bed. By standing, achingly, on tiptoe and by handcrawling himself the last few inches, he could just reach the windowsill and with one desperate sweep sometimes secure something there. Usually it was a caterpillar green and narrow. Like every other living form, to him it seemed incommunicate. The first few he caught he killed with pulling fingers while he tried to understand them. He tasted them. They were bitter—and silent. He felt ashamed and defeated. He caught others and put them back on the bedroom wall where they climbed back to the window. If he had had food with him, he would have tried feeding them. He did try feeding the oval, armoured wood-lice he found beneath rotting leaves in the garden from the egg cup of raisins his mother gave him when she bundled him up in the autumn, in the mornings, closing the gate behind him, while she cleaned house. Unlike the ducks, the woodlice were interested only in running away. He had no string to bring them back. They preferred darkness to whatever light he could offer.

All children are frustrated by the recalcitrance of nature — the puppy which will not be patted, the hamster which hides. For him, the woodlice were an additional puzzle because of the stories. Every night, after tea, his mother took him on her lap and read to him. It was the moment in his day above all others which was understandable to him, one where he lived in coherent companionship and liberty. There, horses, ducks, rabbits, foxes and other animals talked, had adventures and were friends. His mother read well. She read slowly and clearly. She let him see the book as she read and since she re-read the same books many times, he came to memorize the story on each page, cued by the illustration on it or on the facing page. And knowing the story before the story was told was security, power, delight and beauty.

The books she read from, as he came to understand much later after they had vanished into that world of childhood books once possessed and then irretrievably lost, made a strange and culturally displaced collection. They were given to him by his grandmother and step-grandfather who owned an antiquarian bookshop. The books were probably unsellable remnants. He remembered many of them as disbound, with loose pages. They were not modern. The Victorian books were illustrated by black and white steel engravings whose elaborate detail invited close inspection and repelled it at the same time. The animals in these engravings often had a sinewy anatomical accuracy which frightened him more than encountering the animal in the actual would have done. The illustrations he liked best were in what he came to realize, when he saw examples of them again, the Edwardian and immediately post-Edwardian books. They were rich, ornate, highly stylized colour plates, often tipped-in on their pages. They were influenced by the Pre-Raphaelites, by Edward Burne-Jones, by Böcklin, Klimt, Beardsley, by Russian icons, Japanese woodblock prints and Persian miniatures. Many years afterwards when he first saw the stage designs and costumes for the Diaghilev ballets, he recognized again the world of those illustrations. For him, because of the books, that world was never unreal or merely decorative; it was the world of unconditional unpremeditated belief possible in childhood, a world in which metaphors are never concealed similes.

There were other odd books given to him by his grandparents. They contained no stories. They were books of cartoons, French and English, almost certainly late nineteenth-century reproductions since the originals would have been valuable. He would recognize some of their creators when he was much older, Gillray, Rowlandson, and Daumier. Some of the cartoons lampooned the circle of the Prince Regent, later George IV (flatulent, blob-bosomed ladies in seam-split empire dresses, red-coated, whey-faced or scarlet-faced fops and fox hunters, primping in hand mirrors or spewing onto tables littered with knocked-over bottles and decanters). One of the books of cartoons lampooned the Buonapartes, Napoleon I abandoning Egypt, with a smiling Sphinx in the background, mounted on a camel with a face like the Empress Josephine's, Napoleon III, rat-faced and morbidly-waxed-mustachioed, looking as if he had spiders on his breath, surrendering to spike-helmeted Prussians at Sedan. As a child he could not understand the cartoons, but he was pulled back to them again and again, perhaps by their cynicism and violence, until the books containing them were broken apart and scattered. He remembered the cartoons as a child will remember what he does not understand, in fragments. He would remember them when he read the excoriating lines on civil misrule and treachery in the poems of Yeats and Geoffrey Hill a long time afterwards. He remembered them in a sense before he remembered them, just as he read by sight before he could read.

Just so he read the story of the one-legged tin soldier

standing at attention, useless rifle shouldered, in the cocked-hat boat of newspaper, being swirled down a sewer and challenged by a rat four times the soldier's size, a durance all the more terrifying because he was the tin soldier and therefore the rat could only be one of the monsters four times his own size he would have to find the courage eventually to face. And as the tin soldier, he was swallowed by a fish. (In Greece twenty years away, he would dream he was swallowed by a whale and then vomited up on shore — he felt the scrape of the whale's spleen where he woke, still dreaming, to find himself clasping the ankle of a young woman dressed in green.) And as the tin soldier, he was consumed by fire in a stove while a paper dancer flew to perish beside him.

So also he read by sight the story of Bre'r Rabbit and the Tar Baby and saw the Tar Baby sitting on its log as silent as a woodlouse, as impervious to speech, and he felt the Tar Baby gum his fingers, hands and arms in black fluid while it smiled, smiling emptily in a strangling vacuity.

And there was a third image he eventually recovered to look at again in the only one of his childhood books he was able to recognize and acquire when he grew older. It was in Edmund Dulac's *Fairy-Book: Fairy Tales of the Allied Nations*, published in 1916. By then he knew Dulac not as a translator, editor and illustrator of fairy stories but only as the friend of Yeats who wrote music and designed the scenery, costumes and masks for Yeats's Noh play *At the Hawk's Well* which was performed for the first time in a London drawing room in 1916. Dulac was working on the play the same year the *Fairy-Book* was published. Dulac would continue his artistic collaboration with Yeats by carving the counterfeit medieval woodcut portrait of Giraldus, the supposed source of Yeats's cosmological and historical speculation in *A Vision* (1925), and Dulac made other illustrations for that book, including a woodcut of a leaping unicorn.

In the Dulac illustration the child remembered and the man rediscovered, a youth, dressed in a Russian fur-trimmed tuque, an embroidered Russian blouse, purple tights and soft leather fur-lined boots is mounted on a flying chestnut horse. The horse is caparisoned with a floral saddle cloth. The horse's mane of light beige flies upwards like flames. The rider is turning sideways in his bucket saddle to kiss a princess leaning out of an arch of a cupola topping an onion-domed tower decorated with coloured tiles and panels showing images of the moon, sun, stars and planets painted in gold. The hair of the princess is covered by a tall crown inset with rubies and emeralds. Her body is covered by a flowing caftan of light mauve edged by a band of black velvet embroidered with gold flowers. Far below the chestnut horse, its young rider and the princess, is a crowd gathered in a square. The faces of the crowd are so far away they are featureless and a town stretches around them as a collection of onion-domed churches and white, mauve and yellow houses looking as small as beehives.

The story illustrated is "Ivan and the Chestnut Horse." In it, the father of three brothers — one, two, three — dies.

His dying wish is that the three brothers take equal turns for three weeks to read prayers over his grave. But the brothers learn immediately after their father's death that Princess Helena the Fair has just enthroned herself at the top of the tallest of towers and will marry only the suitor who can leap on his horse to where she sits and kiss her in passing as she bends from her throne.

The two older brothers both decide they will win Helena. With a mixture of pomposity, prevarication, condescension, moral bullying and hypocrisy, they manipulate their youngest brother, little Ivan, into carrying out alone the full three weeks of the prayer vigil they all promised their father. The two older brothers use the time they thus secure in primping themselves and training their powerful horses to jump higher. While they are away competing for Helena and failing to win her, Ivan continues praying over his father's grave. Suddenly the unfairness with which he has been treated and his longing simply to see Helena the Fair and the horses jumping cause him to weep.

His father rises from the grave, comforts and praises Ivan, promises to help him win the Princess and with one great shout, two great shouts, three great shouts, summons a beautiful, magic chestnut horse which gallops to circle them once, twice, thrice. His father tells Ivan to enter the horse's head by the right ear and leave by the left, and after Ivan has done so he becomes a man and rides on the horse to Helena's tower. There, he and the chestnut horse leap once, not high enough, twice, not quite high enough and thrice to kiss the Princess whom, of course, he marries, and the chestnut horse gallops away to leap up to or be snatched by a rainbow. Sonnet IV in the second part of Rilke's *The Sonnets to Orpheus* concerns the existence of a similar animal, the unicorn. The second stanza of the sonnet in Stephen Mitchell's translation begins: "It hadn't *been*. But from their love, a pure/beast arose ..." The story "Ivan and the Chestnut Horse" makes truth, as we say in casual speech, and speak truer than we know.

Am I the child who heard his mother speak the truth of that story and who looked at Dulac's illustration for it so intently that he would remember it for the rest of his life? Thomas Taylor, the Neoplatonist, contemporary of Blake, Coleridge, Keats and Shelley, all of whom he influenced (as he was to influence Yeats also) wrote, "... a vision is symbolical of union between the perceiver and the thing perceived." Ivan enters the head of the chestnut horse. If that is so, the child I have been writing about is myself. Or perhaps I am a variation on the theme of the man he might have become living in another country, during a time which can only become less and less his own. Or perhaps my relationship with the child is not that of a variation on a theme but that of the theme itself played by two flutes, one of them me, two flutes waving out and away towards some other minute particular as yet unborn, that will survive as an antique possibly antic cosmology, three wooden ducks in a row.

EPILOGUE

Nay by S. Jamy, I hold you a penny,
a horse and a man is more than one, and yet not many.

THE TAMING OF THE SHREW

Let knife leave the wood. Let
    wood be this wooden man
dancing. He is dancing between
    summer's last light
and the first winter light of November.

Let him leap with his face to light.
    Let him lift up to fall
to lift up again. His dance
    sounds the sound of the ground.
He is gravity's friend.

His leap strikes root into earth.
    He dances the legend that dance
preceded word. He's inscribed
    in no circle. He's not Leonardo's
circumscribed lord.

His body and mind move freely
    together. His left hand
is empty to cape his sleeve.
    His right holds a stick
to sling up and catch

and sling up again a cross-tied
    shuttle of wool as if it
were himself, dancing
    the dancer himself
dancing, fore step, back step

single step, leap. How his weight
    hangs lightly upon him,
no more than a shuttle of air,
    hop back step, cross back step,
shuffle back, leap.

So his dance takes us, no flute
    or fiddle heard, for love makes him
dance, for love of it dance
    as we move with like measure,
our form therein, by love's revealing known.

The frontispiece reproduces an aquatint, *John Stokes' Horse*, made in 2007 by the Newfoundland artist David Blackwood. The size of the original is 16 × 20 inches. For generous permission to use this image, I am deeply grateful to David Blackwood and Emma Butler of the Emma Butler Gallery, St. John's, Newfoundland. Mark Bennet of St. John's photographed the original for use in this book. Blackwood saw the original toy horse in the small museum in Wesleyville, on Bonavista Bay, Newfoundland.

⏳ ACKNOWLEDGEMENTS

The sectional epigraphs are quoted from the following works:
Frederico Garcia Lorca, "In Praise of Antonia Mercé, La Argentina," from *In Search of Duende*, edited and translated by
C. Maurer (New York: New Directions, 1988); W. B. Yeats,
"On a Picture of a Black Centaur by Edmond Dulac," from
The Collected Poems (London: Macmillan, 1979); Roberto Calasso, *Literature and the Gods* (New York: Knopf, 2001); Adam
Zagajewski, "Subject: Brodsky," from *Eternal Enemies* (New
York: Farrar, Straus & Giroux, 2008); and William Shakespeare, *The Taming of the Shrew*, III:ii. "Handle" was written
in the margin of Rilke's "Der Tod" ("Death"). the handle was
found in John Thompson's garden in Jolicure.

I also wish to thank Marie Law, Amanda Jernigan and John
Haney. Some of the poems and an earlier version of "Leaping Time" were first published in *The New Quarterly*. Several
other poems appeared in *Arc*. "Sea Horse" was republished in
The Best Canadian Poetry in English, edited by Lorna Crozier
(Toronto: Tightrope Books, 2010). — P S

This book is typeset in a digital revival of ELECTRA, a sprightly American book type designed by W.A. Dwiggins (1880–1956) and first issued for use on Linotype's metal-casting equipment in 1935. Dwiggins had a significant influence upon the way twentieth-century America looked in print. As well as designing type for Linotype, he wrote the influential book *Layout in Advertising* (1928) and contributed to the design of over 300 books for the New York publisher Alfred A. Knopf. —AS

Gaspereau Press acknowledges the support of the Canada
Council for the Arts and the Nova Scotia Department of
Communities, Culture & Heritage.

Typeset by Andrew Steeves & printed offset and bound
under the direction of Gary Dunfield at Gaspereau Press,
Kentville, Nova Scotia.

7   6   5   4   3   2   1

National Library of Canada Cataloguing in Publication

Sanger, Peter, 1943–
John Stokes' horse / Peter Sanger.

Poems.
ISBN 978-1-55447-113-3

I. Title.
PS8587.A372J65 2012   C811'.54   C2012-900747-1

GASPEREAU PRESS LIMITED ❦ GARY DUNFIELD &
ANDREW STEEVES ❦ PRINTERS & PUBLISHERS
47 Church Avenue, Kentville, Nova Scotia, B4N 2M7
www.gaspereau.com

BOOKS BY PETER SANGER

· POETRY ·

1983 *The America Reel*. Pottersfield Press.
1991 *Earth Moth*. Goose Lane Editions.
1994 *The Third Hand*. With Thaddeus Holownia. Anchorage Press.
1995 *Ironworks* (Letterpress edition).With Thaddeus Holownia.
　　　Anchorage Press. Trade edition in 2001.
1997 *After Monteverdi*. Harrier Editions.
2002 *Kerf*. Gaspereau Press.
2005 *Arborealis*. With Thaddeus Holownia. Anchorage Press.
2006 *Aiken Drum*. Gaspereau Press.

· PROSE ·

1986 *Sea Run: Notes on John Thompson's Stilt Jack*. Xavier Press.
1990 *As the Eyes of Lyncaeus: A Celebration for Douglas Lochhead*.
　　　Anchorage Press.
2001 *"Her Kindled Shadow …": An Introduction to the Work of Richard
　　　Outram*. The Antigonish Review Press. Revised 2nd ed. in 2002.
2002 *Spar: Words in Place*. Gaspereau Press.
2004 *Walden Pond Revisited*. With Thaddeus Holownia.
　　　Anchorage Press.
2005 *White Salt Mountain: Words in Time*. Gaspereau Press.
2007 *The Stone Canoe: Two Lost Mi'kmaq Texts*. With Elizabeth Paul
　　　and Alan Syliboy. Gaspereau Press.
2007 *Laminæ*. With Thaddeus Holownia. Anchorage Press.
2010 *Through Darkling Air: The Poetry of Richard Outram*.
　　　Gaspereau Press

· EDITOR ·

1995 *John Thompson: Collected Poems and Translations*.
　　　Goose Lane Editions.
2001 *Divisions of the Heart: Elizabeth Bishop and the Art of Memory and
　　　Place*. With Sandra Barry and Gwen Davies. Gaspereau Press.